AF448029

UNDERSTANDING THE BASICS OF EBOOK PUBLISHING

IFY EVANGEL OBIM

Copyright © 2021 IFY EVANGEL OBIM

All rights reserved

The characters and events portrayed in this book are fictitious. Any similarity to real persons, living or dead, is coincidental and not intended by the author.

No part of this book may be reproduced, or stored in a retrieval system, or transmitted in any form or by any means, electronic, mechanical, photocopying, recording, or otherwise, without express written permission of the publisher.

ISBN: 9798713123833

Cover design by: Art Painter
Library of Congress Control Number: 2018675309
Printed in the United States of America

This book is dedicated to the Lord Almighty.

CONTENTS

FOREWORD

In as much as there are many books on Electronic Publishing, there is always room for more, especially when such a book is targeted at developing countries. This book is an introductory text on the Understanding of the Basics of Electronic Publishing.

The author, Mrs. Ify Evangel Obim is a Lecturer at the University of Nigeria Nsukka, and have had some years of experience in handling of the course 'Book publishing' adding to the fact that she underwent a course on E-Publishing with the organization 'Write-For-Me' up to the advanced stage. She is therefore qualified and prepared to write this basic material for students and lecturers of tertiary institutions in developing countries.

The author has stated that the book is about understanding the basics of electronic book publishing. She has purposed at helping students and lecturers understand how to write a strong and purposeful book as well as how to go to KDP to publish eBooks the basic and advanced way. She has essentially succeeded in meeting this aim.

She wrote having in mind of lecturers teaching students hence she discussed the topics in a way that will be easy for students to understand. The addition of a worksheet at the end of the entire book also helps the students in summarizing their understanding of the art of electronic publishing. This book is highly recommended to high college students, undergraduates, postgraduates, lecturers, librarians and every other person interested in writing and publishing their books.

Mrs. Chidimma Vivian Mbajiorgu
March, 2021

PREFACE

Printing costs are significantly higher than those involved in publishing on-line because of actual paper and printing costs. Another disadvantage to print publishing is the time that it takes. Not only does the writing and editing take time, but time must also be allotted for the printer. However, being printed also indicates a problem in itself. With a text that must be finalized by the printing press on paper, the final product is relatively unchangeable.

In such a situation, there is an urgent need to look at alternative method of publishing which will eliminate these issues or handle them to a great extent. Hence introducing online publishing or EBook Publishing. But with on-line publishing, there is a much greater amount of ease in editing. If a date is wrong, a word misspelled or tense out of place, a simple correction can be made to the file and updated on the Web.

This book is therefore intended to provide the Basic Method of eBook Creation and Publishing; how to open your Kindle Direct Publishing (KDP) Account with Amazon at no cost; how to publish your Class/Lecture notes using your KDP account; how to write a strong and purposeful book; how to go to KDP to publish your eBooks the basic and advanced way.

This book is therefore intended for undergraduates, postgraduates, lecturers, librarians, high college students, every profession and everyone who in one way or the other will be involved in the publication of their textbooks, novels, Christian books and books in general. The book is organized in such a way as to provide the user with the understanding of the basics of electronic publishing.

Mrs. Ify Evangel Obim
March, 2021

THE CONCEPT OF WRITING

Writing is a form of human communication that includes the use of symbols to express ideas, feelings, and language. Writing is carried out in a systematic manner. Writing improves our capacity to communicate and clarify our thoughts to others and to ourselves. An urge to scribble one's ideas, emotions, and stories arises in this way. Writing is the act of recording one's thoughts and experiences. Writing is the act of bringing words, ideas, and thoughts into print. It is the act of documenting and presenting innovative concepts in a specific order for others to read and be influenced by. Electronic Publishing or EBook Publishing comes after a writing process. Writing therefore can be defined as putting an idea and information down in a constructive manner that enables both the writer and the reader to profit in a way that can outlast them. Also, writing is the act of putting down an idea or piece of information in a more positive way that will help both the writer and the reader in the long run. It is the product of imagination.

Writing is an important communication ability. Effective communication requires good writing skills. It is critical to reference what others have written on the subject matter while writing. It might be necessary to paraphrase (write someone else's ideas and facts in your own words) or direct quotation (write an author's idea verbatim) in some cases. It is important to acknowledge the author of the work you consulted during your writing exercise in all of these ways. Failure to do so constitutes a serious academic crime known as Plagiarism, which translates to "intellectual theft." Plagiarism is when you take someone else's intellectual work or concept and pass it off as your own without properly citing or respecting the original source. Plagiarism can be both deliberate and accidental.

Plagiarism is regarded as a type of intellectual theft or fraud in academic settings. This immoral and deceptive behavior can result in disciplinary action, including expulsion. As a result, since plagiarism is a form of intellectual theft, it is a punishable offense. Plagiarism is rampant in today's digital world, where copying, editing, and pasting other people's work without proper attribution and referencing has become all too simple. The flood of information available on the internet has made it easier to plagiarize other people's work without properly citing it. Plagiarism can be described as the act of copying and pasting material from a source without enclosing the text in a quotation mark and without acknowledging the original author. Without acknowledgment, paraphrasing or summarizing anyone else's job or concept or using a previously submitted work as if it were a new one. This is referred to as self-plagiarism. A writing could be said to be strong.

STRONG WRITING

Strong writing is a writing to fulfill both the writer's and intended audience needs. It is also written to meet the audience's needs and interests to the extent that they are able to pay for it. Strong writing may be an act by which writers relate or express ideas and respond to specific circumstances by means of written words that strike their readers interest. Here the keyword is "strike interest" of the reader. It simply means that there are no boring moments in a novel, and that every word piques the reader's interest. There will be no boring moments if the writing is good. It doesn't mean you have to write an action-packed story in the strictest sense, but it does mean that something must happen in every chapter, and there must be a "cliffhanger" at the end of each chapter to keep your reader interested. It encourages readers to keep reading by arousing their emotions. It also leaves a deep and lasting impact on both the writer and the reader's minds. A strong book or piece of writing goes beyond meeting literary needs to meet the literary needs of the target audience, to the point where they are willing to pay extra money to get a copy for themselves.

MAKING YOUR WRITING UNIQUE

How strong is your writing? How appealing is your message? Think deeply about that as you write. Nothing is really new, but then everything is renewable to adapt and appeal to needs and desires of individuals. Your message, yes, your write-up needs to be strong enough to appeal to your target audience! So, how then do you create a strong writing? The tips below could help you develop your ideas into a strong writing and appealing writing.

1. **Build Your Ideas**: How far or well you go with your writing depends on how good you work on your ideas. Quote me penning down this, 'if your dreams aren't big enough to keep you awake at night, then you're yet to dream, so the moment an idea comes to your mind, build it into something bigger and better and not just verbatim of an existing idea that could bore a reader.

2. **Visualize Your Audience**: Before you begin your writing, have in mind whom you're writing for to ensure that everything about your writing tailors to the needs of your audience. Remember, you're writing for them and not for yourself.

3. **Focus on Clarity**: This is a very vital point when it comes to writing and it is one of the major reasons why books are edited before publishing. When editing a write-up, remove all non-essential points that may distract or divert attention from the true message and leave your readers confused.

4. **Make Your Packaging Attractive**: Remember how many times, you've been drawn to a particular book at the bookshop or bookshelf? What attracted you to the book? Is it the title, the cover,

the shape, the size or the artwork? Yes, humans are prone to getting attracted by what they see and we subconsciously share with others our satisfaction when we use a particular product, thereby advertising the product. Do not neglect those features that could attract people to your write-up (books, contents etc.) Make wise choice when it comes to your graphics, captions and title! Did you know, there's an App that could do all that for you and more?

5. **Consistently launch and keep Launching**: Yes, don't launch once and relax. All the big brands which you've known since you were much younger and even the ones you know came into existence few years ago have never stopped advertising. Therefore, the launching of your book should not just start and end with one big event and then you relax, hoping to be a bestseller, no, it doesn't' work like that, continue to talk about your book/Content to create more awareness.

WHAT IS A BESTSELLER?

Let us consider a type of writing called Bestsellers. They are popular literature, without strict recourse to Laws or morals in literature. The emphasis is on mass appeal. When we say best seller we are referring to a book/publication that has the highest number of sold out copies in relation to other books in its category within a given time frame. The sales can be much above 20,000 copies sold out within a specified period of time.

TIPS TO WRITING A BESTSELLER

1. **Start with a big idea**: Bestsellers are built on big ideas. Not just some old thing regurgitated in a new way. It is something interesting. You must find an idea that will get readers excited to pick your book. This goes for fiction, nonfiction, advice, how-to, educational and memoir. A small idea for a book results in small sales and a big idea will result in big sales. J.R.R. Tolkien spent years developing the languages upon which his entire world was later built. Do not overlook the importance of nailing a big idea before you begin writing and don't rush the research.

2. **Write with the Audience in mind**. Before you start writing,

think about the audience first. Write as though you are writing to answer a question in their minds. The book needs to be written in a way that it can be easily shared and talked about, because it touches on some universal theme. In other words, don't just write a book for yourself. Stephen King says 'you write the first draft with the door closed and the second draft with door open' that is good protocol.

3. **Edit for Clarity, Not for Perfection:** Bestsellers are clear. Take out all the clutters that distract your reader from the true message. Editing is not about making the book grammatically perfect (if that were true, books would be typo free). Rather, it is the process of making your book into what it is supposed to be. So every time you edit your book, ask yourself, "Is this helping what I am trying to say, or hurting it?" Also get someone to proofread and edit. Two heads are better than one.

4. **Package your Book to Spread**: Packaging is about perception. Bestsellers are packaged to sell. The title, cover page and design are all optimized to help the message spread. The way people experience your book will affect how well the book sells and how far it spreads. Your goal is to not only get this thing into people's hands; it is to give them something they want to share. Packaging includes title, cover, artwork, design, etc.

5. **Launching is Key**: Never stop launching. Bestsellers are perennial. The all bestselling books of all time typically didn't come out the gates as immediate successes but because of their timeless nature, they just kept selling. Book launches are great, but you're going to need more than one big event to sell. Understanding the three unique launch phases of a book will help you sell the first 1000 or so copies, but it won't help you sell your next 10,000 or 100,000 copies. The best way to do that is to never stop launching. You just have to be talking about it for a long time. Keep advertising, discussing and referring to it.

    Jeff Bezos initiated the eBook and is the founder of Amazon. He was an ordinary employee @ Macdonald flipping burgers, and worth US$0 because wages couldn't even feed him well. But because of his firm believe in himself and his dreams, he founded Amazon in 1994 @ his garage in Seattle, USA after several many failed attempts. By 2020, he was worth over US$153 billion, and was said to be the richest man on earth according to Forbes. Keep believing in yourself and in your dreams. Be 100% focused, committed, dogged and determined to succeed whatever the challenges that you are encountering or that you might encounter along the line. Nothing good comes easy.

NINE (9) WAYS TO BECOMING A GOOD WRITER, ACCORDING TO BRAD STULBERG.

Write Every Day.
Even if it's only a single paragraph. Even if it's a single sentence! Perhaps more than any other endeavor, I've found consistency essential to developing as a writer. Set aside a time each day, even if it is only 15 minutes to write.

Read Every Day
As you do, note what you like about certain passages (replicate these things) and note what you don't like about certain passages (avoid these things).

Exercise Every Day
My best work from ideas for articles to paragraphs to sentences- always seems to pop into my mind in the midst of physical activity. Consider exercise a part of your job.

Sleep with a Notebook

During big writing projects, I often wake up in the middle of the night with ideas worth exploring-sometimes even entire paragraphs –in my head. I quickly jot them down in a notebook I keep on my nightstand so I can fall back asleep without having to worry about holding onto the idea.

Develop a Routine

I write at the same time, out of the same places (a few neighborhood coffee shops) with the same drink snacking on the same thing. I do everything I can do to offset the uncertainty- the terror-of the blank page.

Don't Write and Edit at the Same Time

When you write just write. Getting stuff out of your head and unto the page is hard enough. Don't make it impossible by trying to do it elegantly the first time around. My routine is straightforward: I write in the afternoon; edit the prior afternoon's work the following morning; and then later resume writing again later in the day.

Stop While You're Ahead.

If you have been writing for more than 90 minutes and the going starts to get rough-stop! Trying to "force it" is almost always unproductive. Plus, if you end on a positive not it's easier to pick back up on positive note.

Work and Re-Work and Re-Work Some More.

It's damn near impossible to get anything right the first time, or the second time, or even the third time. Accept that you –like just about every other writer- need to work like a craftsperson. Chiseling away at a sentence isn't something to get frustrated about. It's something to embrace. Also, read your work out loud. Doing so is the best way to get out of your own head, something integral to making sure that your work makes sense to others.

Write for Yourself First

If you find what you're writing interesting, you'll do a better job writing about it and your audience will find it interesting, too.

THE 97% AND 3% THEORY?
This theory explains how people react to the various elements in the economy;
1. **MONEY**
97% are looking for ways to spend their money while 3% are looking for ways to invest their money.
2. **JOBS**
97% think a better job will make them rich while 3% know that investing is what makes you rich.
3. **RISK**
97% avoid risks because they think about failure. While 3% know that the greatest successes are the fruits of the greatest risks.
4. **PROBLEMS**
97% try to avoid problems While 3% see the problem as an opportunity to win.
5. **PREPARATION**
97% are getting ready for today. While 3% are getting ready for tomorrow.
6. **TIME**
97% are wasting their time While 3% see time as their most valuable asset.
7. **FEAR**
97% are always afraid of losing money while 3% know that if they don't lose money, they can't be wiser, smarter and stronger.
97% see themselves in a comfort zone, they are satisfied with their present earnings while 3% will always look for more, always looking for Opportunities and never see themselves in a comfort zone.
The world trains us to be in 97%. But each of us has the choice of being with the majority or with the minority. What percentage of the human race do you belong to? Be amongst the elite.

TIPS TO CREATING A GOOD CONTENT

Through our writing, we create our content. Content generally means the things contained in something, therefore the content of anything at all is dependent on what that thing actually is.

With this in mind, you may pause and ask yourself, am I a content creator? Did you find answers to your question? I guess you said no, or perhaps yes or you're not sure if you are or not.

The first tip is, **know what you want to write about**, the second tip is, **leave out the topic and develop your article**, your topic can come after your write-up is complete, though if you are writing a story, depending on the category, you may need to write a tagline/logline and then develop your story around that without digressing.

The third tip to help you build or develop your content is **being sensitive and paying attention to details around you**, if you are to neglect this point, you will find yourself struggling to develop a content but hence you're observant, you will discover the great author in you. The fourth tip is, **have a target audience in mind**. Having a particular group of people whom you hope to appeal will help you to choose a language that those category of people will understand better; using a language they understand will also attract and glue them to your content.

If it did, the fifth tip is **"start"**. Yes, get your pen and paper, your notepad or mobile device and start putting down those ideas into writing. The sixth tip is **"write ideas as they flow and stop writing when you find yourself struggling with your write-up.** When an idea comes to your mind, put it down in writing, as ideas flows, you will write them down with ease but trying to write while thinking of what to write may make you struggle with the article you're writing on. When you find yourself at this stage, "take a break" and continue when the ideas starts flowing again.

Once you've been able to develop your content, give it an attractive title. Your title needs to be appealing in order to attract your audience and ensure that the body has a persuasive call to action points driven home for readers' benefit, then you can become a very resourceful author. So what else do you need to become a content creator/ an author? Document your helpful thoughts and ideas and author them to solve other people's problem while benefitting from that.

TIPS TO WRITING

To write a Bestseller, some or all of the following should be done or taken note of:

1. Creating your characters and story line or outline
2. Research
3. Write
4. Edit
5: Effect corrections

WHEN YOU WANT TO START WRITING:

1. Start with a big idea. Bestsellers are built on a big ideas.
2. Start immediately
3. Belief that you have something valuable to say.
4. Write with the audience in mind. Bestsellers are sticky. ...
5. Capture the readers' attention with your opening lines
6. Bookworm your way to success (cultivate the habit of reading i.e. be a reading role model). Hear the following: "If you stuff yourself full of poems, essays, plays, stories, novels, films, comic strips, magazines, you automatically explode every morning like Old Faithful. I have never had a dry spell in my life, mainly because I feed myself well, to the point of bursting. I wake early and hear my morning voices leaping around in my head like jumping beans. I get out of bed quickly, to trap them before they escape."
—Ray Bradbury

"I never desire to converse with a man who has written more than he has read."
---Samuel Johnson

7. Be in the company of like minds (authors) as its usually said 'show me your friends and i will tell you who you are'

8. Edit for clarity, not perfection

9. Package your book to spread (great marketing strategy lies in good packaging)

10. Never stop launching.

11. Never stop trying and keep pushing

WHEN TO STOP WRITING:

1. **When you feel like stopping**
2. **When writing becomes a struggle**
3. **When you feel like increasing the content of your writing**
4. **When you feel like adding just anything and everything into your writing, then pause.**

WHAT IS A BOOK?

A book may be described as a non-periodic printed publication with at least 49 pages (not including cover pages). A book is a collection of intellectual work on any topic organized in a formal order and published or printed in a bound volume with a protective cover.

BASIC PARTS/SECTIONS OF A BOOK.

The front cover, the body (intellectual part) of the book, and the back cover are the three pieces of a book. A more detailed look at a book is as follows:

1. The front matter (cover page/ title, copy right page, dedication, epigraph, prologue, acknowledgements, table of contents)
2. The interior (this is the body/chapters of the book)
3. The back matter (the blurb/about the book and the about the author)

SECTIONS OF A WELL ACCEPTABLE BOOK

1. Title/cover page
2. Copy write page (the authorization given to the author)
3. Barcode (bar codes are found at the back cover of a book, basically at the rear after the author's biography.)
4. Dedication page: where the writer tells the reason for which the book was written

5. Acknowledgement page (talks about all those that assisted to making the book a reality

6. Epigraph, prologue etc.

7. Table of content (a guide to the various chapters contained in the book)

8. Introduction (written after all the chapters have been completed and not before). It is the chapter that talks about the entire book

9. The interior (the body)

10. The back matter (the writer writes to give a short description about the book (blurb), about the author (biography))

11. ISBN/ISSN this number is patented to a particular book. In essence, ISBN is assigned to a specific book.

*Blurb or about the book is a short description about the content of the book. *About the author is a short description or biography of the author written in the third person format e.g. The author is, she is, they are, she works at etc.

What then makes a good book are the following:
1. The quality of the content
2. The need the book addresses or the solution the book proffers. i.e. the solution the book gives or offers.

INTRODUCTION TO E-BOOK PUBLISHING

Electronic publishing is simply a new branch of the publishing industry in which literature is published in a digital format that must be accessed in specific ways rather than in print form with physical pages. E-publishing, or electronic publishing, is a relatively new method of disseminating books, short stories, collections, and nonfiction works via the Internet and computers in general. For topical searches, the word "electronic publishing" is also known as "e-publishing," "digital publishing," "desktop publishing," "internet publishing," and "internet publishing." (Velmurugan & Natarajan, 2015) Electronic publication can be accomplished in a variety of ways. Digital copies of authored books are now distributed by proprietary e-reader designs like the Amazon Kindle or other designs by Barnes & Noble, Sony, and others, according to traditional conventions for e-book publishing. There are also a variety of digital magazines and newspapers that can be accessed through the Internet or downloaded to computers or mobile devices. E-book creation and publishing is a high income skill that would ever be needed at this time and age because of its extensive personal and extended benefits. Everything is practically going electronic, so why not books too!

WHAT IS AN E-BOOK?

Could this be the first time you've come across the word eBook? EBook simply means "Electronic book and this is a publication made available in digital form or soft copy readable in most electronic devices. It consists of texts, images or both as an author deem fit to, to appeal to its target audience. Simply put, E-Book means Electronic Book. E-Book is writing and publishing through electronic media/ medium instead of hard copy or as an extension of the hard copy to reach a wider audience. It is a book in electronic format that is not physically handled. E-book literally means "electronic book," or a book that is read electronically rather than physically. It is a book that is written and distributed using electronic media/medium instead of or in addition to hard copy in order to reach a larger audience. E-books are electronic versions of printed books that can be read on computers, tablets, and other electronic and handheld devices such as smart phones, laptops, and so on. E-books are digital books that contain text, pictures, and animations and can be read on a variety of electronic devices.

WHAT IS A PAPERBACK?

Paperback is a book published in print form with soft cover. Paperback is a book that is bound with a soft paper covering as opposed to hard cover binding. Paper back to an extent can be said to be the opposite of the eBook in the sense that you can physically see and hold the book unlike the eBook that you can only access digitally.

HOW TO CREATE AN E-BOOK
INTRODUCTION TO FORMATTING:

What is formatting? Formatting is the visual style of a document e.g. fonts, borders, etc. Format (formatting) is the layout of your document in a presentable manner. It is an accepted pattern or layout regarding a written document. It guides you in building your book in preparation for your E-Book creation and Publishing.

The term 'formatting' in this context means setting your work to the standard acceptable in the digital platform you wish to publish or simply put 'setting a write-up to the standard acceptable by Kindle Direct Publishing (KDP). This standard has to do with size and layout because not following the set standard could make your publication to be rejected by the application, thus not getting published.

To get started with formatting your publication, follow the simple steps below:

1. Open Microsoft word document and set your page and margin to 6" x 9"
2. Choose your desired styles
3. Format the chapters.
4. Fix your readymade cover
5. Create your pages
6. Fix headers and footers
7. Add images if available
8. Add Table of Contents
9. Double check and convert to PDF.

The next step after the above steps is to create a KDP account, before you do that ensure you have an email address that is still functional, an email address whose password you still remember.

COMPONENTS OF A BOOK

1. Cover page
2. Copyright page
3. Dedication and Appreciation pages
4. Preface
5. Table of contents
6. Body (or Chapters).
7. Back page

Cover Page: This is the first thing you see on a book, yes that beautiful graphics containing the book title and the author's name is the cover page, remember to make it appealing! The cover must be captivating!!!! Some people assess the worth of a book by its cover, so you need to create an enticing cover such that no one will overlook it amongst others. Yes, this is necessary to make the book attractive.

Copyright Page: This page protects the ownership of the writer and tell a reader to what extent they can use the content of the book and whom to seek permission from before using it. Copyright abuse is a very serious crime punishable by law, try not to abuse it. Copyright is the protection of ownership rights to the contents of the book. The information written in any book in the copyright page states the extent to which you can use the contents and who to contact before usage. Copyright abuse is a great crime all over the world. It can cost you money and your freedom - imprisonment if infringed upon.

Dedication and Appreciation Pages: This is the page where the writer gives credit to all who has contributed to the success of their work. Are meant to boost reception and recognition of the book and materials used besides others.

Preface
Is an introduction to a book, typically stating its subject, scope, or aims.

A foreword
Is a section at the beginning of a book that introduces the book and is usually written by someone other than the book's author. To create your book for publishing, all the above and more should be ready on your system.

Table of Contents: This helps readers to choose topics they wish to read first as this comes with chapter title and page for easy location

Body: Your story or write-up according to how it has been listed in your 'table of contents' page.

Back Page: This contains a brief biography of the author and it is usually centered on his works as a writer. It doesn't necessarily contain other information about him not relating to his writing or write-ups. It could also contain information 'about the book'. If it talks about the author, write in the third person pronoun 'he or she'.

Kindle Direct Publishing is an Amazon application that enables you to write, format and publish your work on Amazon. With this application, you can publish your work with ease, using its customized template to format your work or using the App to go through the process. In this lesson, we will learn how to use the customized template to get our works published on Amazon.

WHAT IS A TEMPLATE?

Template is a particular laid down pattern widely accepted, that must be followed when publishing either a hard copy or E-Book.

a template is a physical object whose shape is used as a guide to make other objects.

It is a generic model or pattern from which other objects are based or derived.

It is a chosen or fixed pattern, shape, formula or blue print that serves as a guide for building up other objects.

It is an established formula that can be adjusted to suit ones needs.

It is the accepted style to follow as a guide when putting your books together.

A template is an accepted pattern/layout/model/guide/ formula that is followed in replicating or creating things similar to it. It is a guide that is to be followed to make other things.

BASIC PRACTICAL STEPS TO FORMATTING A WORD DOCUMENT FOR CONVERSION INTO AN E-BOOK

Basic Practical Steps to Formatting:

STEP 1. Set your page and margin. (Trim paper size to 6"×9")
STEP 2. Choose suitable styles and customize same. (Garamond Font style and Font size 11 is acceptable at the Amazon platform)
STEP 3. Format the interiors - Chapters.
STEP 4. Fix your cover designate: Title
STEP 5. Do pagination
STEP 6. Headers fixation
STEP 7. Extras: footers
STEP 8. Add images if available - How?
STEP 9. Table of Contents (TOC)
STEP 10. Proof and conversion from Microsoft Word (MS) to PDF. You're good to E-book!

HOW TO TRIM YOUR PAPER SIZE

To trim to the universally accepted size of 6"×9", do the following:
1. Go to Home Page
2. Click on "Page Layout"
3. Click on Size, above "Page Set Up" to open the dialogue box.

4. Click on "More Paper Sizes" to open up another dialogue box.

5. Adjust Default Paper Size under "Letter" to 6"×9" (width and length).
6. Click Ok.

FORMATING YOUR WORD DOCUMENT USING A CUSTOMIZED TEMPLATE FROM AMAZON:

This template to be used is called CREATESPACE.

Upon manual formatting of your book using the basic formatting method of the createspace template, you open a KDP account at the website **kdp.amazon.com** where you upload and publish your book for the whole world to see within the next 72 hours. Remember, for any book to be published on amazon, it must have a minimum of 24 pages, so when one is planning to publish on Amazon, that should be considered.

FOLLOW THE STEPS BELOW TO CREATE YOUR KDP ACCOUNT.

1. Launch https://kdp.amazo/n.com/en_US in your browser.
2. Click on sign up and enter your details correctly. Please note that this is not a Facebook account where majority of us use funny names to create pages etc. Enter your information correctly and

then click on create to get your account.

3. After that, go to your mailbox and verify your email address to validate your account.

4. Log in to your account to complete your registration by filling your tax and bank information, please fill out all fields correctly and click 'save' at the bottom of the page. Quick tip! Point your cursor or click on any highlighted text around the form to get more information of what should be there.

5. After this, proceed to tax information and fill it out appropriately, and then click save.

6. The next thing is to upload your manually created manuscript and paperback on your KDP account and publish!

HOW TO UPLOAD YOUR EBOOK

Having opened your account you do the following:

Before you follow the six steps below you must ensure that your manuscript is properly formatted according to the Createspace format template which was shared earlier in the Course.

1 Sign in to your KDP account through Amazon (/ kdp.amazon.com)

2. On your account page you will find the Bookshelf (Click on the Bookshelf).

3. Click on CREATE E-Book or KINDLE E-BOOK

4. Create your Cover Page (either using the one you have designed or get a cover page from the gallery).

5. Proceed to the content (Remember that you must have trimmed your paper size to 6" by 9"). Click on "bleeds" if it is a PDF file.

6. Click on "Upload" to upload your manuscript (the system will automatically upload this manuscript and when it has fully uploaded it will preview).

7. Scroll through in the preview pane to confirm that everything is okay.

8. Click on "Publish" once you have ascertained that you are satisfied.

9. After the upload, your paper will come live in 2-3 days (72hours).
The steps listed above is the crux of the matter, the reason we are having this training. The above is the "raison d'etre" of this Basic training.

The above procedure is the basic method of e-Book and paperback publishing while the advanced method uses the Amazon's amazing software that does the formatting of your manuscript, creates/designs the cover page whether colored or plain, prints your eBook in whatever color you want it. All these are done within minutes. This software uploads and publishes your paperback and eBook seamlessly within minutes and books will come out LIVE within next 72 hours of upload.

ADVANCED E-PUBLISHING

Your KDP account is the most important element in the publishing business. So to create your cover,
the following are the process and things you need:
- A customized image, like the one you created or used/ or get any image of your choice.
- an author's image ready
- a concise about the book ready in MS word
- a concise about the author ready in MS word
There are 2 types of images you can use for your cover designs
1. The images on the Amazon gallery
2. Your own images.
You can decide Which to use.
COPYRIGHT INFRINGEMENT
It is when you use an image big time, then they'd invoke the copyright infringement law on you.
Do you also know your books can be unpublished or rejected for publishing by KDP if they noticed the
Contents or images, have copyright issues.
The reason they'd always ask you if you have rights to the contents and images used before
publishing your works. And even when you succeeded at publishing, they may unpublish it.
So be careful. Copyright violation is a serious crime. As far as copyright infringement is concerned,
there's no ignorance in the law courts. Whether you bought

them knowingly or ignorantly, you're liable.

FOR PRACTICAL COVER CREATION USING THE COVER CREATOR TOOL

You'd need these status:

1. Ensure you've published your eBooks to the point of cover creation.
2. Authors image must be ready
3. Any image you need for the front cover - this is optional as you can use from the KDP gallery.

HOW TO GENERATE YOUR KDP PDF PREVIEW PROOF COPY

You can only do this for your paperback publishing.

After uploading your manuscript and cover. The next stage is *preview*.

When you click on preview and it opens, at the top right of the preview page, you'd see,

Download PDF preview copy.

HOW TO EDIT, UNPUBLISH BESIDE OTHERS - A PUBLISHED BOOK

Go to the homepage of your KDP account, which doubles as your homepage.

- go to the particular book
- click the yellow button at the end of the book roll
- it's give you several options, like edit, unpublish etcetera
 Make your choice.

REFERENCES

https://www.techopedia.com/definition/1265/electronic-publishing

Velmurugan, C., & Natarajan, R. (2015). Electronic Publishing: A Powerful Tool for Academic Institutions in the Electronic Environment. *International Journal of Library Science and Information Management (IJLSIM),*

Vol.1(1), 10–18. Retrieved from https://www.research-gate.net/publication/283433308_Electronic_Publishing_A_Powerful_Tool_for_Academic_Institutions_in_the_Electronic_Environment

WORKSHEET
Kindly summarize your understanding of the chapters here.

www.ingramcontent.com/pod-product-compliance
Lightning Source LLC
Chambersburg PA
CBHW071241140726
47996CB00007B/2707